Repeat As Needed

Contents

When I Was Straight	5
Middle School Science Class	6
Dustin Wants To Write A Poem With Caridad	7
(a collaboration with Caridad Moro-Gronlier)	
Furious Cleaning	8
Homophobic Barbie	10
The Almost Never-Ending Villanelle	11
(a collaboration with Beth Gylys)	
Ways To Get Over A Broken Heart	12
Responses To Exes As Three Poems	14
Things that Definitely Suck	15
Bitch Baby Tears Villanelle	17
Presidential Circus Villanelle	18
(a collaboration with Denise Duhamel & Beth Gylys)	
Olivia Benson Barbie	19
Dustin Wants To Write A Poem With Nicole	20
(a collaboration with Nicole Tallman)	
Straight People	22

The Inspirations	26
Notes	27
Acknowledgments	28
Gratitude	29
A Note to Allison Blevins	30

When I Was Straight
After Maureen Seaton's "When I Was Straight"

I stayed home
while my mother
drove to the grocery store.
Two hours alone to prance
in my mother's high heels,
wear her dresses and nightgowns,
and a white t-shirt as a wig.
I'd probe her jewelry box,
slip on a ring or two,
a necklace, and the bracelet
she only wore for special occasions.
Sometimes I even applied
her lipstick with a smile.
I'd sit back straight, legs crossed
directing the household staff
that we didn't have
on the tasks of the day:
vacuum, mop, polish the china,
and press the laundry—
a boss lady before
being a boss lady was a thing.
I'd twirl around the living room
with one hand extended,
an invitation to a man
who wouldn't enter my life
for another thirty-five years.

When I was straight,
my father would say,
*I'd rather one of my sons
blow my brains out
than tell me he's gay.*

Middle School Science Class
Inspired by Denise Duhamel's "Nature"

Mrs. Smeyser explained the life cycle of stars.
Our sun, a yellow dwarf, will become a red giant.
Flames will consume Mercury and Venus
like appetizers before reaching Earth.
My ears ignored the 5-billion-year timeline.
I exclaimed, *We're going to burn to death!*
Mrs. Smeyser laughed, *I don't plan on being around.*
Giggles wafted through the air.
A few students looked as horrified as me.
Maybe they too were Southern Baptists
raised on fearing a city of flames. I knew
God would use the sun for the final destruction.
The red giant loomed. My face red from its heat.

Dustin Wants To Write A Poem With Caridad

After Maureen Seaton & Nicole Tallman's "Nicole Wants To Write A Poem With Maureen"

Dustin is writing this poem hungry. He's on another diet, but he swears he isn't and won't get hangry. Dustin wants to know what Caridad is having for dinner.

Caridad means to tell Dustin she is having grilled chicken and spring mix for dinner, but it comes out as spring chicken and grilled mix. Caridad laughs at the gaffe because it sums up her youth when all she ate was grilled chicken and spring mix—in public, that is. Caridad sighs with resignation when she says, *I got fat anyway.*

When Dustin hears or reads the word fat, he thinks of *Sordid Lives*— how Bonnie Bedelia's character Latrelle removed the husky label from her son's jeans, sewed on a slim label in its place. Dustin's mother used to ask him, *Do you want to be fat like your father's mother?* Then add, *Don't tell your father I said that.*

Don't tell your father, is what Caridad's mother says when they slip into the Orange Julius at the mall for a midday pick-me-up teeming with all the sugar he doesn't allow either of them to have. Caridad's father monitors her mother's weight and dress size which is why her mother bursts into tears when the maroon, size 8 slim-hipped polyester bell bottoms she's been eyeing don't fit her size 10, well hipped body. *Don't tell your father,* she says later at home as Caridad watches her remove a size 8 tag from a Papi approved pair of pants and replace the size 10 tag on the new pair she brought home with it. It is painstaking work that requires tiny snips, a practiced stitch, a lie ever ready on the lips. Caridad never tells.

Furious Cleaning

After Maureen Seaton's "Furious Cooking"

It's the kind of cleaning that begins
with spitting, yelling, and cursing

because you can't believe he—
you— let it get so damn bad.

You inventory the papers, clothes, random
plates, and the lilies he bought to make you smile—

label everything *his* or *mine*.
His is destined for the garbage

bag you open with a fast swoop.
Air doesn't even fill the bag

before you sling the first item inside
looking for the next version of him

while eyeing those fucking lilies.
It's the kind of cleaning

that makes you sweat like working in the yard,
the kind that makes you stop to catch your breath.

The kind that is cathartic like a Sexton poem,
serves retribution like a Dante punishment,

cleanses like bleach on the floor.
I remember my mother standing at the sink

staring into her task of diluting bleach,
then on hands and knees scrubbing

an already spotless floor.
Tears fell from her eyes

as she dipped sponge in water,
mumbled *the bathroom is next*

all while cursing my father's name,
cleaning every spot named Christina.

Homophobic Barbie
Inspired by Denise Duhamel's Kinky

She didn't picket when marriage equality passed,
only asked, *How do you know who the bride is?*
When SCOTUS ruled on workplace discrimination,
she was silent on Facebook, but asked Ken,
Do people really get fired for being gay?
When the assurance to compliance
for the NEA was updated, she huffed,
My trans friends won't mind if I comply.
They can always call me if they're in a pickle.
Homophobic Barbie will tell you
she's had an owner or two turn gay.
(Technically, it was her owner's brothers.)
She knew one was gay when he made Q-tips
into hair rollers. The other
instigated arguments between her and Ken.
Ken had never questioned why he wasn't allowed
to drive the Barbie Convertible across the living room.
Homophobic Barbie loves the sinner, hates the sin.
She isn't sure two dads or two moms
create the best environment for a child
but shows up for the wedding.
She isn't missing an open bar
or chance to do the Electric Slide
in pink heels with her sister Skipper.
After her third glass of champagne,
Homophobic Barbie explains to Skipper,
Remember, in the beginning,
Mattel created Barbie and Ken, not Ben and Ken.

The Almost Never-Ending Villanelle

A contoured villanelle using "How to Do Nothing" by Melanie Weldon-Soiset

I knew, (but didn't) that it was time to get out.
I'd ask myself, *tomorrow or today*?
My head and heart each walk a different route.

How many times did I unpack my suitcase to flout
myself? Shoes back toe to toe with yours, I'd say,
in a whisper, *Is now the time to get out*?

One foot in, one out, a hanging chad, I'd pout
& putz around the house thinking about a way
forward, a diversion, a different route

for my life. I didn't stay because I'm devout,
though, believe me, I've sunk to my knees to pray
asking God, *Isn't it time that I finally get out?,*

dug my nails into my back to draw blood. Throughout
our relationship you've treated me like clay:
something to mold, a stone along the route.

When I slammed the door, I had no doubt
we were done, over, a corpse oozing decay.
Sometimes I hate myself for not getting out,
sticking so stubbornly to that dead-end route.

Ways To Get Over A Broken Heart

Inspired by Carlos Antonio Rancaño's Evidence Or How To Get Over A Broken Heart

I.
Get lost in the woods.
Scream at the trees
and the goddamn birds.

II.
Drive cross-country.
Don't stop for gas.
Finish the journey on foot.

III.
Sob.
Sob until God fears
you'll one up His flood.

IV.
Go to Costco.
Eat samples.
All the samples.

V.
Jump in the deep end of a pool
fully clothed. Sink to the bottom.
Stay until you feel the choke.

VI.
Go to the beach.
Read *The Awakening*.
Never enter the ocean.

VII.
Reach into your chest,
pull out the heart shards.
Drop them in the disposal.
Flip the switch.

VIII.
Remove the remnants
of Cupid's fucking arrow.
Use the art of kintsugi
to meld a stronger heart.

IX.
Repeat as needed.

Responses To Exes As Three Poems
Inspired by Beth Gylys's "Three Poems"

Ex 1
* Block *

Ex 2
All we had was lust.

Ex 3
I'm no longer attracted to broken things.

Things That Definitely Suck
After Andrea Gibson's "Things That Don't Suck"

Iguanas. iPhones that won't hold a charge. Super(wo)man without a cape. Tripping while jumping rope. Morning breath. Curling. (It isn't a sport!) Fortuneless fortune cookies. The movie *Leprechaun*. Empty Amazon boxes. People that ignore welcome mats. Hand-me-down underwear. Train derailments. Clowns. Scratched CDs. Sitting on a needle cushion. Permanent markers washed in laundry. People who vote against caring for our veterans. Forgetting the location of the time capsule. Empty martini glasses. Being bullied during recess. Feeling lost and never found. Squeaky grocery carts. Not enough tambourine. Cigarette ashes. Shipwrecked boats. Beets. Yellow snow. Broken windows. Swing states swinging red. Out of sync dance routines. Burnt mac & cheese. Murder hornets. Being punched. Stuck on a Ferris wheel with a full bladder. Missing buttons. Chipping a tooth. A dust allergy. Misogyny. Hobby Lobby. Duck face. Not being invited to a sleepover. Southern Baptist sermons on tape. Betsy DeVos as your grandmother. Melanoma. Killer algae. Farmers taking advantage of migrant workers. Teenagers practicing bagpipes. The news according to Fox News. Adults shaking children. Putting children in cages. No-talent-kiss-asses that succeed. Dog shit on your new loafers. The Vietnam War. The Iraq War. The "War on Drugs." WAR! Wet mail. The justice never served. Confederate flags waving in the back of a pick-up truck on a Georgia summer day. Being strung along. Fake friends. The phrase: *Boys can't wear pink*. The phrase: *Girls must love pink*. Dead birds. Broken chopsticks. Toenail collections. The electric chair. Sewing without thimbles. Eviction notices. Vaping. The door of opportunity closed because you aren't a cisgender heterosexual white male. Leaky tubs. Grief heavy on your chest. Litter on the playground. No PPE. Being turned down after a flash mob proposal. Bed bugs. Cavities. Blown electrical sockets. A termite infestation. Flat tires. Poison ivy. Systemic racism. The scales of justice tipped in the wrong direction. Op-eds glorifying Trump. Chugging Drano. Sex without lube. Lube without sex. Losing at HORSE against your older brother. Snorting cocaine. Fines for overdue library books. Oatmeal raisin cookies substituted for chocolate chip cookies. Bombs. Slip n' sliding Susan Collins. Republicans with hard-ons for a wannabe dictator. Caterpillars that die before becoming butterflies.

Bitch Baby Tears Villanelle
A contoured villanelle using Beth Gylys's "Fat Chance"

My poems come straight from the heart,
he posts. (If you think cliché, we're a match.)
He brags online about being so smart—

a self-taught poet means an honest start.
No musical beds at conferences. He's no lech.
He writes poems that come from the heart.

He'll tell you quickly his work sets him apart.
No cheating with MFA connections, but attached
to bragging: his success is because he's so smart.

First English major to be a success from Hobart.
Indiana should make him State Poet Laureate. Watch
as he recites a poem written from his heart.

He demands, *Put my books in your online cart*.
Another award he didn't win. A wretch?
No. He's overlooked for being too smart.

He's a poetry soldier continuing his march
into the lives of all readers. You're his match
because he writes every poem from the heart.
Not a fan? Obviously, you aren't that smart!

Presidential Circus Villanelle
A contoured villanelle using "Gratuitous Oranges" by David Shapiro

Life was hard when the president was orange.
His decisions were stained with a greenish tinge.
Some faces nearly froze in expressions of cringe

as trick-or-treaters carved Trump-o'-lanterns, orange
parents attending a MAGA party in a garage.
We held our breath, when the president was orange.

We choked on juice and cursed the harvest moon, orange
& removed our protest signs & rally gear from storage.
Watching the evening news, we'd curse and cringe,

eating Cheetos and Circus Peanuts, an all-out binge
listening to the wannabe dictator discuss ways to impinge
on refugees and lefties, his face so orange,

his white-collar crimes so dirty, not even a *laver le linge*
would cleanse, and he's placed at the hinge
between bad and worse deeds to make us cringe.

We shut off our TVs, our cells, trying to expunge
the xenophobia, & his face, so damn orange.
We were tested when the president was orange—
his citrus squeeze & his mug, an eclipse, so cringe.

(Note: This poem was written during the Biden administration. If this poem had been written during the orange one's second term, given the gross human rights violations and authoritarian agenda, the language would be more urgent, sober, and full of rage.)

Olivia Benson Barbie
Inspired by Denise Duhamel's Kinky

Mattel thought I was clueless about the damn memos
written by male execs when I existed only as a concept:

> *A girl detective goes too far.*
> *What if she empowers girls too much?*
> *Who hasn't forced a Ken on a Barbie?*
> *Can Barbie even say no? LOL!*

After the box office success of *Barbie*,
the suits held an emergency board meeting.
Twenty-five years as a detective
taught me weak men are fucking
afraid. They acted quickly to orchestrate
my Women's History Month release,
gifted pink buttons with #MattelLovesFeminism
and reusable bags with #WomanGetItDone
to employees in the El Segunda headquarters—
entered each in a raffle to win
a first edition replica of me
with my namesake's autograph on the box.

I now patrol playrooms
protecting every Barbie, Midge, and Skipper—
even Bratz and American Girl dolls.
I watch every Allan
with an encroaching stare,
slamming each Ken
with a trespassing hand to the ground,
press my sensible square heel
into the small of his pathetic plastic back.

Dustin Wants To Write A Poem With Nicole
After Maureen Seaton and Nicole Tallman's "Nicole Wants To Write A Poem With Maureen"

Dustin tells Nicole he thought of her the other day when a coworker said: *There's Florida, and there's Miami. They are very different places.* A few weeks earlier, at a Dolly Parton Day event in Nashville, Nicole had said, *It's Miami and the rest of Florida.* Dustin asks Nicole, *What's so damn special about Miami?*

Nicole tells Dustin she thought of him when she saw a billboard of Dolly on the roof of the Velvet Taco. It wasn't just Dolly but also the importance of kindness that made her think of him. Nicole thinks Dustin is one of the kindest people she knows. Nicole wants to tell Dustin what's so damn special about Miami, but she's still trying to figure that out herself.

Dustin's instinct is to argue against the compliment—that's life with a narcissist parent. He (begrudgingly) writes thank you. He considers himself kind, but never nice. He hates when people call him nice. He's really fucking nosy (think Gladys Kravitz on speed), takes pride in being a smartass, and recycling *Drag Race* shade. He can never live a WWDD* life. (*What Would Dolly Do? DUH!)

Nicole's instinct is to challenge Dustin's idea of what it means to be nice. She considers kind and nice to be synonyms, and she thinks nice has gotten a bad rap because it's sexier to be mean than nice. She loves when people call her kind or nice, and she thinks both are the highest compliment. Nicole, however, also has a hard time accepting compliments, but she doesn't really want to talk about her parents today.

Dustin loves a challenge, gladly accepts Nicole's non-challenge challenge. * *He throws the gloves he isn't wearing to the ground* * (It's Miami in August!)   He asks Nicole if they're dueling in this poem. (Is a poetry duel even a thing?) The Betsy Hotel with the live music, the Prosecco chilling by the table, and the Labradors Bee and Rosa walking the lobby is an excellent location for a non-challenge challenge. Dustin wants Nicole to know he loves the comic print on her jacket, her brutal honesty, and her poems. He's going to miss being able to meet her for a drink.

Nicole loves a challenge, but she loves chilled Prosecco and the piano even more right now. She looks away from her laptop and refills her flute. (It's always August in Miami.) Nicole asks Dustin if he wants another grapefruit mimosa. The Betsy Hotel is the place to drink and write poems together. She wants Dustin to know that she loves his Dolly trucker hat, his quick wit, his poems, but she's not going to miss meeting him for a drink and writing together. *Nicole books a flight to Asheville for November.*

Straight People

Inspired by "White People Always Want to Tell Me They Grew Up Poor" by Megan Fernandes

don't like to be corrected.

Sexual orientation,
not sexual preference.

Straight people
love to message us on Facebook
10 to 15 years after graduation
to say:
It's okay that you're gay.
or
I'm proud of you!
or
Yaaaaaas queen!
or
Look at you. You go, girl!

Straight people
love to ask
with a Leslie Stahl stare:
Which one of you is the woman?
When we respond,
we're both guys,
they insist,
But which one of you,
you know, does the woman stuff?

Straight people
love to tell us:
I have a gay friend.

Then they ask,
Do you know him?

And we have to say
a prayer to Dolly Parton
so we don't respond:
Yes, our homo registry
is updated each night
and downloads
while we sleep.
We are Borg.

And they love to close
the conversation with:
Y'all should meet.

>[heterosexual dramatic pause]

You'd be so cute together.

Trans and bi people
never say these things to us.
They too deal
with heterosexual commentary.

Bi people are often teased:
You can't make up your mind.
 or
At least your dating odds
increase by 50%.
or
Why do you have to be so greedy?

Straight people
will tell trans people
remembering pronouns is hard,
forgetting dead names is difficult,
but they will give an oral report
on all eight seasons of *Game of Thrones*

without forgetting or mispronouncing
a single goddamned name.

Straight people
will ask trans people,
Did you have the surgery?
Then point below the waist.

Straight people
will say they love us
and vote for politicians
seeking to strip us
of our rights.

Oh.

Straight people.

Straight people.

Straight people.

The Inspirations

Maureen Seaton's *Little Ice Age* (Invisible Cities Press, 2001), *Furious Cooking* (University of Iowa Press, 1996), & *The Sky Is an Elephant* (ELJ Editions, 2023); Denise Duhamel's *Girl Soldier* (Garden Street Press, 1996) & *Kinky* (Orchises Press, 1997); Mariska Hargitay's portrayal of Olivia Benson on *Law & Order: Special Victims Unit*; Melanie Weldon-Soiset's "How to Do Nothing" published in *Untold Volumes*; Andrea Gibson's *Pansy* (Write Bloody Publishing, 2015); Beth Gylys's *Bodies that Hum* (Silverfish Review Press, 1999); David Shapiro's "Gratuitous Oranges" published in *Poetry*; and Megan Fernandes's *Good Boys* (Tin House Books, 2020).

Carlos Antonio Rancaño's *Evidence Or How To Get Over A Broken Heart* is printed to the right with permission. Visit Carlos online at carlosrancano.com.

Scan below for *Repeat As Needed* inspired writing prompts.

Notes

The contoured villanelle takes the end word from each line of an existing villanelle and then matches end words in the same order to construct a new villanelle. (I created this villanelle variation in late 2024.)

In "Dustin Wants To Write A Poem With Nicole," Betsy's name was changed to Bee. (Don't hate me, Betsy. Extra head rubs the next time I see you.)

"Homophobic Barbie" references a change to the National Endowment of the Arts (NEA). In 2025, at the direction of the Trump administration, the Assurance of Compliance page for the NEA was updated to include the following new requirements:
- The applicant will comply with all applicable Executive Orders while the award is being administered.
- The applicant's compliance in all respects with all applicable Federal anti-discrimination laws is material to the U.S. Government's payment decisions for purposes of section 3729(b)(4) of title 31, United States Code, pursuant to Executive Order No. 14173, Ending Illegal Discrimination and Restoring Merit-Based Opportunity, dated January 21, 2025.
- The applicant will not operate any programs promoting "diversity, equity, and inclusion" (DEI) that violate any applicable Federal anti-discrimination laws, in accordance with Executive Order No. 14173.
- The applicant understands that federal funds shall not be used to promote gender ideology, pursuant to Executive Order No. 14168, Defending Women From Gender Ideology Extremism and Restoring Biological Truth to the Federal Government.

Acknowledgments

Grateful acknowledgement is made to the editors & staff of the publications in which poems from *Repeat As Needed* first appeared, sometimes in an earlier version:

Birdcoat Quarterly, "Presidential Circus Villanelle"; *Crab Orchard Review*, "Olivia Benson Barbie" & "Bitch Baby Tears Villanelle"; *Diode*, "Ways To Get Over A Broken Heart"; *Emerge Literary Journal*, "Responses To Exes As Three Poems" & "Straight People"; *FERAL: A Journal of Poetry & Art*, "Dustin Wants To Write A Poem With Nicole"; *Jake Magazine*, "The Almost Never-Ending Villanelle"; *Jet Fuel Review*, "Dustin Wants To Write A Poem With Caridad"; *Mollyhouse*, "Things That Definitely Suck" & "Furious Cleaning"; *Olney Magazine*, "Middle School Science Class"; & *TAB: The Journal of Poetry & Poetics*, "When I Was Straight"; and *Whale Road Review*, "Homophobic Barbie."

Grateful acknowledgement is also made to:

Georgia Poetry in the Parks— a collaboration between Georgia Center for the Book, the DeKalb Library Foundation, & Georgia Poet Laureate Chelsea Rathburn— for featuring "Middle School Science Class."

Braving the Body (Harbor Editions, 2024), edited by Nicole Callihan, Pichchenda Bao, & Jennifer Franklin, for reprinting "When I Was Straight."

Note:

"Furious Cleaning" was published in *Love Most Of You Too* (Harbor Editions, 2021).

"Homophobic Barbie," in an earlier version, was published in *Never Picked First For Playtime* (Harbor Editions, 2023).

Gratitude

Much appreciation to the artist and writers whose works inspired these poems.

Gratitude to Beth Gylys, Denise Duhamel, Nicole Tallman, and Caridad Moro-Gronlier for collaborating. Additional gratitude to Beth & Denise for embracing the contoured villanelle.

Thank you to The Betsy Hotel for sponsoring The Betsy Writer's Room. Thank you to Deborah Briggs for her management of the program. The collaborations with Nicole and Caridad started at The Betsy Hotel bar during my 2023 Writer's Room residency.

Many thanks to Denise, Beth, Emma Bolden, Josh Davis, and my Converse Low-Res MFA workshop peers for their input on some of these poems. Gratitude to Donna Vorreyer for helping me sequence this chapbook. Hugs and gratitude to Emma for always being a sounding board and sharing laughter as a fellow meme queen. Love and gratitude to Diamond Forde for her friendship, support, & infectious optimism. Shoutout to these writers/friends for sharing their light with me: Ben Kline, L.J Sysko, Julie E. Bloemeke, Aaron DeLee, Rachel Hanson, Jason Caudle, & Kristiane Weeks-Rogers. Caridad & Nicole, we're the power of three! Love to Ryan, Ashley, and Merry, and Sissy (AKA John) for their support.

Chris, my best friend and fiancé, thank you for your unwavering support and love. You are my shelter and rock.

A Note To Allison Blevins

As five years of writer's block came to an end, I set off to revise a chapbook that I was ready to scrap. I added a few poems and decided to try submitting the chapbook a few more times. I submitted *Love Most Of You Too* to Small Harbor Publishing's (SHP) first open reading period. Your acceptance email arrived in November 2020 while I was sitting at my dual-purpose kitchen table and office (Covid!). I had entered a phase of self doubt, and your belief in *Love Most Of You Too* was the Cher slap I needed to make me snap out of it.

You started as my publisher, and you quickly became a dear friend. You've championed my writing and treated my poetry with such care. When you accepted this chapbook in early 2024, neither of us knew it would be my last chapbook with SHP. Life had other plans. I've transitioned from a press author to the volunteer role of Operations Director. It's been exciting, educational, and rewarding to work behind the scenes supporting the press that has supported me. Friend, it's an honor to learn from you and build community with you.

Allison, thank you for being such a damn good human and exemplary literary citizen.

I'm lucky to have you in my life. Thank you for being my friend. Thank you for being you. I love you!

P.S. We need to make that 1am, post-Punch Bucket Lit Taco Bell run full of laughter and spilling tea an annual event.

About the Author

Dustin Brookshire (he/him) is the 2024 recipient of the Jon Tribble Editors Fellowship and author of the chapbooks *Repeat As Needed* (Harbor Editions, 2025), *Never Picked First For Playtime* (Harbor Editions, 2023), *Love Most Of You Too* (Harbor Editions, 2021) and *To The One Who Raped Me* (Sibling Rivalry Press, 2012).

He's the co-editor of *Let Me Say This: A Dolly Parton Poetry Anthology* (Madville Publishing, 2023) & editor of *When I Was Straight: A Tribute to Maureen Seaton* (Harbor Editions, 2024).

Dustin's poetry has been published or is forthcoming in *Five Points*, *Pleiades*, *South Carolina Review*, *Jet Fuel Review*, and other publications. He's been anthologized in *Divining Divas: 100 Gay Men on their Muses* (Lethe Press, 2012), *The Queer South: LGBTQ Writers on the American South* (Sibling Rivalry Press, 2014), *Braving the Body* (Harbor Editions, 2024), and *Invisible Strings: 113 Poets respond to the songs of Taylor Swift* (Ballantine Books, 2024).

Dustin resides in Asheville, NC, with his partner Chris and cat Jude Paw.

More at dustinbrookshire.com.

About Small Harbor Publishing

Small Harbor Publishing is a 501c3 nonprofit organization. Our goal is to publish unique and diverse voices. We are a feminist press, and we are committed to diversity and inclusion. We strive to bring new voices to a devoted and expanding readership.

Small Harbor Publishing began in 2018 with the first issue of *Harbor Review*. The magazine is an online space where poetry and art converse. *Harbor Review* quickly grew and now publishes reviews and runs multiple micro chapbook competitions, including the Washburn Prize and the Editor's Prize.

In July 2020, Small Harbor Publishing was officially incorporated and began Harbor Editions. Harbor Editions accepts submissions through a chapbook open reading period, a hybrid chapbook open reading period, the Marginalia Series, and the Laureate Prize.

In 2023, Harbor Anthologies began with a mission to promote texts that explore social justice issues and highlight marginalized writers.

If you would like to support Small Harbor Publishing, visit our "About" page at: smallharborpublishing.com/about.

www.ingramcontent.com/pod-product-compliance
Lightning Source LLC
Chambersburg PA
CBHW051705040426
42446CB00009B/1311